Best Wishes!

Shelly S. Hammond

IN MY MOTHER'S GARDEN

Illustrated by Shelby S. Hammond

GIBBS·SMITH PUBLISHER

SALT LAKE CITY

97 96 95 94 93   10 9 8 7 6 5 4 3 2 1

Published by Gibbs Smith, Publisher
Peregrine Smith Books
P.O. Box 667, Layton, Utah 84041

Design by Leesha Gibby Jones

Heather Bennett, Editor
Lynda Sessions Sorenson, Editor

Printed in Hong Kong

Library of Congress Cataloging-in-Publication Data

Hammond, Shelby S.
    In my mother's garden: Illustrated by Shelby Hammond.
       p.   cm.
  ISBN 0-87905-5618
    1. Mothers—Poetry.
  I. TITLE

ACKNOWLEDGMENTS

David Huddle, "THE FRONT YARD," from *Stopping by Home.*
Copyright © 1988 by David Huddle. Reprinted by permission.

Maurya Simon, "From DAYS OF AWE." Published by Copper Canyon Press.
Reprinted by permission of the author.

Phyllis McGinley, "From THE ADVERSARY," from *Times Three.*
Copyright © 1959 by Phyllis McGinley. Reprinted by permission of
Viking Penguin, a division of Penguin Books USA Inc.

Contents

❧ *S. E.—Celia Thaxter* *1*

❧ *THE FRONT YARD—David Huddle* *3*

❧ *From TO MOTHER—Anne Campbell* *5*

❧ *From TO A LITTLE INVISIBLE BEING WHO IS EXPECTED*
   SOON TO BECOME VISIBLE—Anna Barbauld *7*

❧ *TO MY MOTHER—Thomas Moore* *9*

❧ *From DAYS OF AWE—Maurya Simon* *11*

❧ *From POEM IN OCTOBER—Dylan Thomas* *15*

❧ *IN MEMORY OF MY MOTHER—Patrick Kavanagh* *17*

❧ *OUR MOTHER—George Eliot* *21*

❧ *HER GARDEN—Freda Downie* *23*

❧ *DEAR OLD MOTHERS—Charles S. Ross* *27*

❧ *From THE ADVERSARY—Phyllis McGinley* *31*

❧ *HEIRLOOM—Kathleen Raine* *35*

❧ *TO MY FIRST LOVE, MY MOTHER—Christina Rossetti* *37*

❧ *MY MOTHER'S INFLUENCE—Estelle Harte* *41*

S. E.

She passes up and down life's various ways
With noiseless footfall and with serious air:
Within the circle of her quiet days
She takes of sorrow and joy her share.
In her bright home, like some rare jewel set,
The lustre of her beauty lives and glows,
With all the fragrance of a violet,
And all the radiant splendor of a rose.
As simple and unconscious as a flower,
And crowned with womanhood's most subtle charm,
She blesses her sweet realm with gentle power,
And keeps her hearth-fires burning clear and warm.
To know her is to love her. Every year
Makes her more precious and more wise and dear.

—*Celia Thaxter*

THE FRONT YARD

The main difference between yard and lawn
is a yard has crabgrass, dandelions, holes, bumps,
and ruts, while a lawn is smooth. In ours, moles
made sure what we had was a yard. Mother
desired a lawn, though, and called it that. Her
lilacs and forsythia dreamed along
with her, but honeysuckles grew over
our fence, up our porch lattice, and clover—
better for us than for the farmers it bloomed.
Ours was a yard all right. Now I ease
the dark and cold out of this northern winter:
I dream a boy with mason jars for bees,
both honey and bumble, hummingbirds never captured,
and lightening bugs for when it's late in my dark room.

—David Huddle

From TO MOTHER

You are the golden link between the days
Of happy, careless childhood, and this hour.
Because of you I know green woodland ways
And quaint old country gardens burst in flower.
There will be meadowlands where children run
And daisies lift shy faces to the blue;
There will be brooks that sparkle in the sun
As long as I have you!

—Anne Campbell

From *TO A LITTLE INVISIBLE BEING*
WHO IS EXPECTED SOON TO BECOME VISIBLE

She only asks to lay her burden down,
That her glad arms that burden may resume;
And nature's sharpest pangs he wishes crown,
That free thee living from her loving womb.

She longs to fold to her maternal breast
Part of herself, yet to herself unknown;
To see and to salute the stanger guest,
Fed with her life through many a tedious moon.

Haste little captive, burst thy prison doors!
Launch to the living world, and spring to light!
Nature for thee displays her various stores,
Opens her thousand inlets of delight.

—*Anna Barbauld*

TO MY MOTHER

They tell us of an Indian tree
Which howsoe'er the sun and sky
May tempt its boughs to wander free,
And shoot and blossom, wide and high,
Downward again to that dear earth
From which the life, that fills and warms
Its grateful being, first had birth.
'Tis thus, though wooed by flattering friends,
And fed with fame (if fame it may be),
This heart, my own dear mother, bends,
With love's true instinct, back to thee!

—Thomas Moore

From *DAYS OF AWE*

The click and shiver of memory haunt me.
What is printed inside the roots of a tree

remains a mystery to me, as does the shape
of death astride its white stage, or the lake

under which our ancestors sleep stacked
like spoons. I look at your paintings backed

against the walls and feel my heart repair itself.
Your every touch is lyric, your embrace felt

even by the wilted purple zinnias in the room.
At night I watch your colors step from their two-

dimensional tombs to raise the rooftop.
Don't let fame's twisted face taunt you now,

nor the concatenation of years chain you to the past:
your genius waltzes alone in the cathedral's vast

worship; alone, completely alone, undaunted.
Today the sun blooms like a poppy, and the taut grid

called heaven is awash with brilliant stars.
Sixty leave-takings, sixty greetings, sixty years!

Mother, listen: your paintings speak to us
about how absence itself, is a wondrous house.

—*Maurya Simon*

From POEM IN OCTOBER

Forgotten mornings when he walked

with his mother

Through the parables

Of sunlight

And the legend of the green chapels.

—Dylan Thomas

IN MEMORY OF MY MOTHER

I do not think of you lying in the wet clay
Of a Monaghan graveyard; I see
You walking down the lane among the poplars
On your way to the station, or happily

Going to second Mass on a summer Sunday—
You meet me and you say:
"Don't forget to see about the cattle—"
Among your earthiest words the angels stray.

And I think of you walking along the headland
Of green oats in June,
So full of repose, so rich with life—
And I see us meeting at the end of town

On a fair day by accident, after
The bargains are all made and we can walk
Together through the shops and stalls and markets
Free in the oriental streets of thought.

O you are not lying in the wet clay,

For it a harvest evening now and we

Are piling up the ricks against the moonlight

And you smile up at us—eternally.

—Patrick Kavanagh

OUR MOTHER

Our mother bade us keep the trodden ways,
Stroked down my tippet, set my brother's frill,
Then with the benediction of her gaze,
Clung to us lessening and pursued us still
Across the homestead to the rookery elms
Whose tall old trunks had each a grassy mound,
So rich for us we counted them as realms
With varied products; here were earth nuts found
And here the Lady-fingers in deep shade,
Here sloping toward the moat the rushes grew,
The large to split for pith, the small to braid
While over all the dark rooks cawing flew—
And made a happy strange solemnity
A deep-toned chant from life unknown to me.

—*George Eliot*

HER GARDEN

My grandmother grew tiny grapes and tiger-lilies,
But there is no sentimental cut to her garden
Through a fat album or remembered lane;
Only interior voyages made on London ferries

Paddling the Thames' wicked brew to Silvertown,
Where regular as boot boys, the factories
Blacked her house every day, obscured the skies
And the town's sweet name at the railway station.

Between ships parked at the end of the road
And factory gates, she kept her home against soot,
Kept her garden colours in spite of it—
Five square feet of bitterness in paved yard

Turned to the silent flowering of her will,
Loaded with dusty beauty and natural odours,
Cinnamon lilies, and the vine roots hanging grapes,
Sour as social justice, on the wash-house wall.

—*Freda Downie*

DEAR OLD MOTHERS

I love old mothers—mothers with white hair
And kindly eyes, and lips grown soft and sweet
With murmured blessings over sleeping babes.
There is something in their quiet grace
That speaks the calm of Sabbath afternoons;
A knowledge in their deep, unfaltering eyes
That far outreaches all philosophy.

Time, with caressing touch about them weaves
The silver-threaded fairy-shawl of age,
While all the echoes of forgotten songs
Seemed joined to lend sweetness to their speech.

Old mothers! as they pass with slow-timed step,
Their trembling hands cling gently to youth's strength.
Sweet mothers!—as they pass, one sees again
Old garden-walks, old roses, and old loves.

—*Charles S. Ross*

From THE ADVERSARY

A mother's hardest to forgive.
Life is the fruit she longs to hand you,
Ripe on a plate. And while you live
Relentlessly she understands you.

—Phyllis McGinley

HEIRLOOM

She gave me childhood's flowers,
Heather and wild thyme,
Eyebright and tormentil,
Lichen's mealy cup
Dry on wind-scored stone,
The corbies on the rock,
The rowan by the burn.

Sea marvels a child beheld
Out on the fisherman's boat,
Fringed pulsing violet
Medusa, sea-gooseberries,
Starfish on the sea-floor,
Cowries and rainbow-shells
From pools on the rocky shore.

Gave me her memories,
But kept her last treasure:
'When I was a lass,' she said.
'Sitting among the heather.
'Suddenly I saw
'That all the moor was alive!
'I have told no-one before'.

That was my mother's tale.
Seventy years had gone
Since she saw the living skein
Of which the world is woven,
And having seen, knew all;
Through long indifferent years
Treasuring the priceless pearl.

—Kathleen Raine

TO MY FIRST LOVE, MY MOTHER

Sonnets are full of love, and this my tome
Has many sonnets: so here now shall be
One sonnet more, a love sonnet, from me
To her whose heart is my heart's quiet home,
To my first Love, my Mother, on whose knee
I learnt love-lore that is not troublesome;
Whose service is my special dignity,
And she my lodestar while I go and come.

And so because you love me, and because
I love you, Mother, I have woven a wreath
Of rhymes wherewith to crown your honored name:
In you not fourscore years can dim the flame
Of love whose blessed glow transcends the laws
Of time and change and mortal life and death.

—*Christina Rossetti*

MY MOTHER'S INFLUENCE

Soft, feathery flowers of blue
Were in my garden border set.
Beside them, clothed in tender green,
Grew the dear, fragrant mignonette.

I plucked a spray of blossoms blue,
And kept them with me in my room.
And presently I'came aware
Of faintest fragrance from their bloom.

I wondered what it might mean,

That such a fragrance I should get

From the scentless flowers,—until I thought,—

They grew beside the mignonette!

So haply from this life of mine
May come a spreading fragrance yet—
I surely should some grace have caught—
I grew beside thee,—Mignonette!

—*Estelle Harte*